Customer Service 101

Using common sense to provide a superior customer experience

Bob Copper

Self Storage 101

866-269-1311

Copyright 2012

Birmingham, AL

Contents

Customer Service

'Viewing your customers as the most important part of your job and having a sincere appreciation that they choose to do business with you'.

No matter how busy you are you will only get one chance to make a first impression. Make it a good one.

What is Superior Customer Service?

The self storage professional knows that superior customer service does not necessarily mean addressing customer complaints; superior customer service means using learned skills to keep customer complaints from happening.

Self storage customers need the services of a self storage facility because something has happened: death or birth, marriage or divorce, upsizing or downsizing, business expansion or business closing, moving in or moving out.

Whatever the reason it is normally stressful and the self storage manager that can exercise superior customer skills to reduce the stress and anxiety of their customer can garner a larger share of the self storage market. How you handle people really does matter to the success of your storage facility.

You may believe that having only a few customer service issues from time to time 'isn't bad' and in the overall work experience at your facility, maybe it's not.

But for each of those tenants who have a bad customer service experience their particular circumstance may represent a 100% failure rate in their eyes. Never minimalize a customer's service issue.

Why is Superior Customer Service so important to your business?

A recent Customer Service survey indicates:

- People will spend up to 10% more for the same product with better service.
- We tell from 9 to 12 people when we get good service.

- We will tell up to 20 people when we experience poor service.

Providing Superior Customer Service is good for business.

What Does The Customer See?

It is important to think like a customer when you operate your facility. You'll then be making choices that are attractive to customers and will maximize the value of your services. Ultimately, this will maximize your income, increase facility value and grow your reputation as a professional.

Regarding offering the highest levels of customer service, consider:

- Are your cameras, monitors and recording devices operating properly?

  - If a customer sees blank monitor screens or missing 'squares' on the multi-screen camera display, what message are you sending about your security measures?

- Are your restrooms clean and well stocked?

  - Many retail and service industry customer service industry surveys indicate that one of the first things customers check out at a business is the cleanliness of the restrooms.

- Are lights working and are elevators in good working condition?

  - Consistently leaving burned out light bulbs in place or not replacing ballasts that are going bad creates safety and confidence issues.

  - Your level of customer service drops dramatically if you don't keep your elevators clean and in good working order.

- Is your rental truck clean and full of gas?

  - Make sure you clean out your truck and fill it with gas after every rental return.

- Are you consistently open when your office hours say that you are?

  - Superior customer service means arriving a few minutes before opening time and being ready for customers as soon as the door opens.

  - You tell customers they are not important if you are consistently missing when the office is supposed to be open.

- Do you keep promises and return phone calls?

  - Not doing what you promise to do means you don't care about customers or your facility.

  - Your customers deserve your attention and your respect enough for you to return their phone calls.

- Are leaks fixed and doors repaired in a timely manner?

  - Your customers expect you to keep the property well-maintained and to use reasonable precautions to keep their goods protected.

- Is your rental process quick and simple or long and cumbersome?

  - Do you keep in mind that your customers are likely going through a stressful time when they contact you about storage?

  - Are you organized in such a way as to make your lease process smooth and stress-free?

Being proactive about reducing or eliminating potential customer service issues will increase your level of customer service. Superior customer service means eliminating potential problems, not fixing them after they become problems.

What is Your Customer Service Attitude?

Conduct a self evaluation of your customer service attitude by asking these questions:

- When speaking to a customer do you give him or her complete attention and avoid doing other activities?
    - o Or do continue to work on the computer, text on your phone or work on your crossword puzzle?
- Do you make eye contact with a customer to show that you are paying attention?
    - o Or do you look past the customer with disinterest?
- When speaking on the phone do you make an effort to use inflection in your voice to convey interest and concern?
    - o Or is it clear that the customer is an interruption of whatever you were doing?
- If you have to put someone on hold do you ask his or her permission?
    - o Or do you tell them you are going to do it anyway?

- Do you avoid industry-speak terms and use language the customer can understand?
  - Or do you assume everyone knows what 'climate-control' and 'keypad access' are?
- If you cannot provide the exact product or service a customer needs to you suggest options or alternatives?
  - Or are you so rigid in your offerings that you have no flexibility?
- Do you sincerely apologize to a customer when a mistake has been made by you or the company?
  - Or do you place blame?
- When a customer does complain do you remain calm and understanding, even if you believe the customer is wrong?
  - Or do you try to out-argue the customer or try to make the customer believe their complaint 'isn't' that big of a deal'?
- Do you see complaints as an opportunity to improve service?
  - Or as a problem that is taking up your valuable time?

Learn to Communicate

The self storage professional creates an atmosphere of the expectation of superior customer service by communicating that expectation to their customers. Your ability to effectively communicate with your customers will help you reduce potential customer service issues before they become issues.

There are various means by which you can more effectively communicate to your customers to enhance their customer service experience. Some of those ways are verbal while some are non-verbal.

A recent study was done on how people receive messages from other people:

- 55% of what we learn from others comes from their body language.
- 38% comes from the tone of their voice.
- 7% comes from the words they say.

Body Language

Clearly body language is an important aspect of how we communicate to our customers. The primary ways in which we communicate through body language are:

- Eye contact
    - o Do not look away if you want to show you really care.
- Facial expressions
    - o This is your 'billboard' that lets everyone around you know what kind of mood you are in.
- Body posture and movement
    - o To show you are intently listening to and interested in a conversation with your customer remember to nod, face the customer and lean forward.
- Hand gestures
    - o Whether you use your hand a little or a lot the important thing is to be natural in your movements.

- Touching
  - The most acceptable form of touching is a firm handshake.
- Physical distance
  - Try to be sensitive about maintaining a safe personal zone so you more easily facilitate communication, comfort and trust.

Voice Tone

Almost the entire message you project to a customer over the phone is communicated through your tone of voice and it does not take long for customers to pick up on your attitude.

- A monotone and flat voice says 'I'm bored and I don't care'.
- Slow speed and low pitch says 'I'm depressed and want to be left alone'.
- High pitched and emphatic says 'I'm enthusiastic!'
- Abrupt speed and loud tone says 'I'm angry!'

You will only get one chance to make a great first impression. To improve your tone of voice:

- Smile when talking on the phone
  - People can tell if you are smiling and people prefer to deal with happy and friendly people.
- Practice stressing your words
  - Make sure your tone is clear and your words are easy to understand.
- Breathe: deep, long and slow
  - Take your time and don't rush the call.

Learn to Listen

- Listening carefully to the customer will give you ideas on how they think, what they feel to be important, and why they are saying what they are saying.

- Effective listening puts you in a far better position to effectively identify and develop a plan for their needs and ultimately provide the best service.

- Customers will clearly tell you what is important to them and what their expectations are if you would just pay attention to what they are saying.

Learn to Smile

- Whether you are talking to a customer on the phone or in-person, using your best smile means a great deal whether you are renting a unit, taking a payment or discussing a past due account.

- Become more aware of your facial expression when a customer comes into your office. A smile works much better than a frown and customers can often judge your mood on how you look when they approach you.

- People like doing business with friendly people that know how to smile! A customer's first impression of you should be that you are friendly.

It is also important to ask for and then use a customer's name in your conversations. People love to hear their name and your use of their name communicates that they are important to you.

Let them know you want to help

No matter a person's need or request your natural response should be 'I can help you with that!' Your customers want to know that you genuinely care and you are willing to help.

Ask good questions

When you are trying to assess someone's needs or customer service issue ask good questions to make sure you clearly understand their position.

By asking good questions you establish your sincerity. It is important that after you ask questions that you then carefully listen for the answer.

If you are distracted or feign interest in a customer's need or concerns it will be apparent to them.

Make it a habit to make good notes when asking questions. This insures you are focused on the answers and you are more likely to not forget what the customer said.

Under promise and over deliver

- Providing great customer service means always doing what you promised, and then doing more than the customer expected.
- Do it quicker, better, cheaper, or at a higher quality that the customer would have ever expected.
- Customers are more likely to remember the extra service you delivered than they are the original customer service issue.

Handling customer complaints

Don't take it personal when a customer complains. Think of a complaint as an opportunity to get valuable feedback from your customers.

Customer complaints must be dealt with sympathetically, calmly and promptly. If you follow these standards you will be able to diffuse a customer's feeling of disappointment, anger and embarrassment.

There is an 82% chance that customers will repurchase or remain a customer from you if their complaint is handled quickly and pleasantly.

You may not be able to make it go away, but you can certainly *"make it better"*!

Customer Basic Needs

Your customers have six basic needs they are looking for as it relates to customer service issues:

- Friendliness
  - o Your ability to treat any customer service issue with a sincere smile will go a long ways towards addressing the problem.
- Understanding and Empathy
  - o The more you listen and pay attention you will communicate that you really do understand and are empathetic with the customer's concerns.
- Fairness
  - o Oftentimes managers tend to promise more than is necessary to fix a problem. Customers simply want to be treated fairly.

- Control
    - o Ask your customer how you can best address their problem and listen to their solution. They will appreciate that you considered their idea to solve the problem.
- Options
    - o Customers are much more likely to accept a 'no' if you also offer options that can still address their problem.
- Information
    - o Clearly communicating why or how something might have happened and then clearly explaining how the issue will be addressed is an important aspect of providing superior customer service.

When a customer is upset and has a complaint they want two things: they want to express their feelings and they want their problem solved.

Customer Service Tips

Listen

- Listen calmly and empathetically. Do not interrupt the customer. Do not look away or appear to be distracted. Give the customer your complete attention.
- Nod your head frequently.
- Maintain eye contact.

Be empathetic

- I can see why you feel that way
- I see what you mean
- That must be very upsetting
- I understand how frustrating this must be
- I'm sorry about this

Apologize

- Phrase apologies in terms of being sorry that the customer has been disappointed. Do not state or imply that there is a fault or that service has been bad. When you apologize, MEAN IT, after all customers are VIPs

Clarify

- When appropriate, repeat the facts of the customer's complaint back to them ensure you fully understand the problem.

Explain

- Explanations of what might have happened or why things are done as they are must be clear and favorable to other staff and to the organization. Do not attach blame in your explanation.

Agree

- Gain agreement from the customer about the next course of action to be taken. Suggest only action and alternatives which are within the organization's policy. Where necessary get help from a supervisor.

Take Action

- Prompt action, within organization policy must be taken. This applies as well when that action is to get a supervisor to assist you. Nothing aggravates customer's more than unnecessary delay in resolving their complaint.

Driving a Customer Crazy

If you treat your customer like an adversary and it is clear that you are not interested in seeking ways to help resolve the customer's issue you will drive your customers crazy. To avoid driving customers crazy avoid using these phrases:

- That's not our policy.
- That's not my job.
- I'm not allowed to do that.
- I have no idea.

And you can really add to the craziness if you use these body language signals:

- A blank stare
- Head held down
- Look-away eyes
- Derestricted fidgeting

The key to providing superior customer service is to ask yourself 'What does the customer need and how can I provide it to the best of my ability?'

Specific Customer Service Steps:
While every self storage facility has different customer service steps that need to be taken to move their service level from good to great, there are six common steps that every facility can take to enhance the customer service experience:

- Answer the phone promptly
  - Within three rings with a smile
  - Be clear and friendly
  - Offer your name and ask for theirs

- Return customer calls in a timely fashion
  - Meet or exceed the customer expectations and keep your promises.
  - Even if you don't have the answer to their problem call and tell them you don't yet have the answer.

- Be attentive to your customers
  - My eye contact with customers
  - Shake hands
  - Stand up when they come into the office
  - Meet them at the door

- Be empathetic with an upset customer
  - o Always apologize if a customer is upset.
  - o Ask good questions and listen

- Take responsibility for helping a customer
  - o Always give the customer your name and your best contact number.
  - o Tell them the date and time you will get back to them with an answer to their issue.

- Dress appropriately for work
  - o Look like the self storage professional the customer contacted to solve their problem.
  - o Shave and practice good dental hygiene.
  - o Wear clean and pressed clothes.

Ten Customer Service Do's and Don'ts

- Never say 'I don't know' but instead say 'I'll find out.'
- Never say 'No' but instead say 'What I can do is...'
- Never say 'That's not my job' but instead say 'This is who can help you'.
- Never say 'You're right, this stinks' but instead say 'I understand your frustration'.
- Never say 'That's not my fault' but instead say 'Let's see what we can do about this'.
- Never say 'You need to talk to my manager' but instead say 'I can help you.'
- Never say 'You want it by when' but instead say 'I'll try my best.'
- Never say 'Calm down' but instead say 'I'm sorry'.
- Never say 'I'm busy right now' but instead say 'I'll be with you in just a moment'.
- Never say 'Call me back' but instead say 'I'll call you back.'

Handling Difficult Customers

Handling an angry customer

1. If a customer is angry, never get angry back. It can only turn an unpleasant little incident into an unpleasant big incident.
2. Do not try logical argument on a customer in a tantrum: it only adds fuel to the fire.
3. Do not grovel, and do not let an angry customer draw you into accepting his assumption that the organization is generally inefficient because of his own single unhappy experience.
4. The way to deal with an angry customer is to apologize for the specific inconvenience only, and to take immediate action to put it right.
5. An angry customer means that you still have an opportunity. If the customer storms out of the office, (or slams down the phone), never comes back, and tells all his or her friends/colleagues that it's a dreadful place, that's real damage.

But if the customer comes to you in a temper, you have the opportunity to prevent that damage - the real disaster has not happened yet, and if you handle the situation correctly, it won't happen.

Handling a chatter box

1. Never show your boredom or frustration. It will offend other people as well as the chatter box.
2. Never bully or hector any customer, or interrupt rudely, or shut them up by visibly trying to dominate them.
3. When dealing with a compulsive talker, use every conversational gap and lead that you can to guide the conversation towards a satisfactory conclusion.

Handling a rude customer

1. Do not get personally upset by the rudeness of an offensive customer. And do not fuel his/her abuse by making 'value judgments', just stick to facts.
2. Do not be deliberately casual or icily superior to show an offensive customer what you think of him.

3. The way to deal with the offensive customer is to keep cool, keep your professional detachment, stay polite, and keep offering possible solutions in strictly factual terms.
4. Learn to ignore rudeness. Remember that the offensive customer is offensive to everyone who deals with him/her, not just you. Your job is not to make him/her nice; you simply have to supply him/her with what he/she came for.
5. It is worth recalling the point that you do not have to make an angry person into a nice person. That's impossible. All you have to do is to get them to go away with whatever it was they came to get.

The very difficult customer

Sometimes you do everything right. You've put all the right techniques into practice, but the person remains difficult. In this case, you should try to bear in mind that:

a. Difficult people are usually difficult for a reason.
b. People who are scared and anxious are most likely to be difficult - and may remain difficult until their problems are resolved.

Anxious people can become childlike and have "tantrums". Treating them like children will encourage them to act like a child, while treating them like responsible adults will encourage them to act rationally

e.g. *"I understand your problem and I assure you I'm trying to help. Please take a seat and I will let you know as soon as I have any information ".*

will be much more calming and effective than:

"I am doing all I can. You will just have to wait your turn ".

If people remain angry, it is often because they think that they are not being listened to.

- Make an effort to look as if you are interested. Put your listening skills into practice.
- Particularly difficult people may be playing to the crowd.
- Try to take noisy and unreasonable people aside - perhaps to a separate room or waiting area.

- You may gain the sympathy of other people when dealing with difficult customers. These sympathetic people may try to help by arguing with or commenting on the behavior of the difficult person.
- While this may feel like welcome help, remember that it is easy for the difficult person to feel even more threatened and aggressive.
- A desk can act as a barrier.
- It may help to stand side by side with a difficult customer in a quiet place.

Famous Customer Service Quotes

1. The goal as a company is to have customer service that is not just the best but legendary. *Sam Walton, Founder of Wal-Mart*
2. Your most unhappy customers are your greatest source of learning. *Bill Gates*
3. It is not the employer who pays the wages. Employers only handle the money. It is the customer who pays the wages. *Henry Ford*
4. Well done is better than well said. *Benjamin Franklin*
5. Spend a lot of time talking to customers face to face. You'd be amazed how many companies don't listen to their customers. *Ross Perot*
6. If you do build a great experience, customers tell each other about that. Word of mouth is very powerful. *Jeff Bezos, CEO Amazon.com*
7. Customer satisfaction is worthless. Customer loyalty is priceless. *Jeffrey Gitomer*
8. Quality in a service or product is not what you put into it. It is what the client or customer gets out of it. *Peter Drucker*
9. Customers don't expect you to be perfect. They do expect you to fix things when they go wrong. *Donald Porter, V.P. British Airways*
10. Good service is good business. *Siebel Ad*
11. One of the deep secrets of life is that all that is really worth doing is what we do for others. *Lewis Carol*

12.   Being on par in terms of price and quality only gets you into the game. Service wins the game. *Tony Allesandra*

13.   You'll never have a product or price advantage again. They can be easily duplicated, but a strong customer service culture can't be copied. *Jerry Fritz*

14.   If you want to lift yourself up, lift up someone else. *Booker T. Washington*

15.   Know what your customers want most and what your company does best. Focus on where those two meet. *Kevin Stirtz*

16.   Loyal customers, they don't just come back, they don't simply recommend you, they insist that their friends do business with you. *Chip Bell, Founder Chip Bell Group*

17.   Make a customer, not a sale. *Katherine Barchetti*

18.   Customer service is not a department, it's everyone's job. *Anonymous*

19.   Make your product easier to buy than your competition, or you will find your customers buying from them, not you. *Mark Cuban*

20.   If you work just for money, you'll never make it, but if you love what you're doing and you always put the customer first, success will be yours. *Ray Krock*

21.   I won't complain. I just won't come back *Brown & Williamson Tobacco Ad*

22.   Every company's greatest assets are its customers, because without customers there is no company. *Michael LeBoeuf, Author of: How to Win Customers and Keep Them for Life*

23.   Every contact we have with a customer influences whether or not they'll come back. We have to be great every time or we'll lose them. *Kevin Stirtz*

24.   Statistics suggest that when customers complain, business owners and managers ought to get excited about it. The complaining customer represents a huge opportunity for more business. *Zig Ziglar*

25.   Profit in business comes from repeat customers; customers that boast about your product and service, and that bring friends with them. *W. Edwards Deming*

About the Author

Bob Copper has worked extensively in the self storage industry for many years, amassing vast experience in effective operational systems, successful marketing initiatives and asset value creation. He has traveled around the country conducting countless due diligence projects, operational audits, market studies and  training assignments within the self-storage industry. Bob is known throughout the self storage industry for his no-nonsense approach to improving operations, profits and values and is sought out for his unbiased and professional opinion in all self storage related discussions.

His consulting firm, Self Storage 101, with offices in Alabama and California, is among the largest in the industry and is recognized as one of the few firms capable of large projects and assignments. His team of professionals has vast experience in development, management, turn-around, and vendor contacts and has a unique understanding of all aspects of the self-storage industry. They also provide industry leading training programs, extensive workshops, up to date manuals and other industry-specific materials.

Bob has a Bachelor's Degree from Stetson University in Deland, FL. He speaks frequently at industry gatherings and has written extensively for industry publications.

Bob can be reached at 866-269-1311 and you can find out more about Self Storage 101 at www.selfstorage101.com.

www.ingramcontent.com/pod-product-compliance
Lightning Source LLC
Chambersburg PA
CBHW071553170526
45166CB00004B/1656